BUILDING LIGHT

MICHAELA BELMONT

Building Light

Copyright © 2020 by Michaela Belmont.

All rights reserved. This book or any portion thereof may not be reproduced or used in any manner whatsoever without written permission of the author except for the use of brief quotations in a book review.

First Edition 2020.

ISBN: 978-0-9995726-4-1 (Paperback)
ISBN: 978-0-9995726-5-8 (Ebook)

Cover designed in 2021 by Fulton Hobbs.

Library of Congress Control Number: 2020909249

Requests for permission or further information can be sent to info@michaelabelmont.com.

www.michaelabelmont.com.

From the bottom of my heart, thank you to everyone who sees the beauty in people and mirrors it back so that they can see it themselves. Thank you to those who show others that they are sacred.

Dedicated to Delaney and Catelyn the Bunny.

- Delaney -

My bestie, my soulmate. Thank you for letting me find you, and for sharing this journey with me. I am grateful that we are together during this very long kindergarten. I love you, soul friend.

- Catelyn -

May you have safe journeys wherever you may go. Let no harm come to you that my love can prevent. I love you, my baby, my little angel.

Contents

I. Stepping Off the Edge of the World

I wiggled free like a tadpole	1
Glass Eye	2
Blue Fire in the Black	3
Someone New	5
At the Mouth of the Cave	6
Moon	7
Night Ocean Waves	8
Everything in Its Time	9
Lilac Over Down	11
Into the Valley	13
Playground	14
Ink and Broken Branches	15
Sand Dunes	16
A Saintly Café	18

II. Emerging Into the Painful Bright

The Mountain	21
Blue Whale	22
Roaring Wooden Waves	23
New Level	24
City of Lights	25
Daylight Ocean Waves	26
Dismantling Black and White Thinking	27
Something Very Plain	29
The Arrival of Rage	30
Blood on the Banks of Tripoli	31
Autumn	32
Ash Storm	33
Ghost	34
A Day in Winter	35
Be Whole	36
Talking About It	37

I Don't Grieve Well	39
Cut Open	40
Withered: Something Else Grew	41
Don't Feel Good	42
Haunting the Cemeteries	43

III. Settling Into New Skin

It Will Get Better	47
Gold and Silver Trees	48
Sailing Home	50
The Sunset Isles	51
To Choose	54
Instar	55
Cracked Open	56
To Teach, and Speak	57
Ruined Temples, a Stolen Childhood	59
Once Her	60
Small Water Worlds	61
Suffering or Nothing	63
Towers Out of Words	64
A Silkie's Defiance	66
Wind Chime	67
Falling Down Through the Floor	69
Door to the Cosmos	71
To Build – A Poem About Light	72
Trying to See	74
It's Okay to Just Sit With It	75
Encased in Glass	77
Journey to the Nightmare Realms	78
Catelyn the Bunny	80
Phoenix From the Deep	82
Preening Geese	84

IV. Afterword

I.

Stepping Off the Edge of the World

I wiggled free like a tadpole

I wiggled free like a tadpole, one little kick and I left my body.
I was gone. Out. Free.

I didn't see any light, only darkness. But that
was all right because it was the comforting darkness …
the darkness of creation.
Of the other places … the old places.
Where it all started, before
the universe had shape and defined edges.

Those things that seemed so physical, so
unchangeable, so *real* … I snapped free of them
with one kick like a tadpole.
They were just dreams, vapors.

I left my body behind.
And I died.

Glass Eye

I finally see it.
That truth I've always been pursuing, that
understanding for which I fingered into open,
excruciating wounds and tongued the bloody
sores left behind by the extrication of painful
memories. Pulled at this always unraveling
thread until it finally led me here.
I see it.
It's so old. And it hurts.
But here it is, this ... truth.
My truth.
Everything I've ever said has been wrong. Every
idea was flawed. This truth stares at me, as
unfeeling and unblinking as the glass eye that
is all that remains of an ancient, withering
stuffed animal
under the bed of a long-forgotten room,
even the reaching sunbeam spilling
out under the blinds coated in dust.
Every adult thought I've had has been a lie.
I haven't known a thing since I was three.
At four I began to unravel, to disintegrate
And I fell
Apart.

Blue Fire in the Black

Blue fire, blossoming in the black.
Serenity, though it wears a heavy, sad cast.
As it billows out toward me, swallowing the black,
I see what I have always seen.
And what I have always tried to forget.

It takes a lifetime of lies to convince yourself
you don't know everything already.
You knew how it all was going to go.
You knew when you were two.

But growing up is moving forward backwards.
You see nothing at all.
And all those things, that you used to know
You start to forget it all.

I'm so tired of believing that I'm insecure, broken,
in need of a father's love.
I control my destiny.
I create my universe.
I am the faceless, all-powerful, omnipotent force
in and around myself.
I am not helpless.

I am God.

Work, computers, cars, trees. This mundane, superficial
world of the physical. I tire of the games.
I tire of pretending to be a flesh and bone creature,
when it is so obvious to me that I am
a wisp, a demon, a spirit made of stardust.
I am billowing blue fire
consuming the black.

When are we all going to stop pretending? That we're flesh and bone.
That this physical world has any sort of reality to it at all.
When are all these spirits
going to stop dreaming?

Someone New

The outer shell is splitting, blood running out the cracks.
Fresh skin, new skin, unfolding out the back.
Curled up, growing pains, growing AGONIES, more like.
I'm becoming someone new.

And oh it hurts.
It hurts and hurts and hurts and
HURTS

At the Mouth of the Cave

The cliché is that the hands are covered in blood.
But mine, mine, are just stained in
dirt.

Centuries have passed me by, and I'm still
standing at the mouth of this cave,
awaiting your reappearance.
Betrayer, betrayer. I call upon you.
This sick, heavy feeling in my gut.
I feel sick, I feel sick.
My eyes have been ever affixed to this place
and to the old scars you left upon my soul.
But there's no movement, or sound. No sign
of anything stirring.

Come out of this cave! I howl, and anger's flip side
is terror.
But I'm not sure if you're even still alive in
there, or if you're as big as I remember.
What if I brave the darkness in there to go
after you …
And you're just a blind grubby beast groping
about in the dark?

What if you're pathetic?
What a waste this suit of armor would have
been.
How embarrassing, all these tears and poems.
If I were to face you, invincible demon of my past,
And find you to be … nothing.
Nothing at all.

Moon

I am a moonlit creature.
Suspended so delicately
this frozen form like marionettes.
Pitch dreams. I watched the ink
descend.

Gazing up with rapt attention
I felt that sense of belonging and freedom
that otherwise eludes me.
It cradled me once again,
and as I rose up I forgot for a time
all the imprisoning and painful things,
including love.
Love is a form of slavery. It chains you to another person.
I have spent most of my life
in chains.

Night Ocean Waves

The roaring waves of darkness, crashing
against our shores. The backdrop against
which our lives are framed.
And those selfish
corpses, bland faces and clawed hands,
swallowed by the ocean, spread sick
on us at night
and then walk on earth during the day.
Ebbing tide reveals
the bones they left behind.
But, covered again, and forgotten
in the to-and-fro of the ocean.

Everything in Its Time

I spoke to an old man down the way who said,
"Everything in its time."
As he said this he looked down at the fresh
green little shoots of plants
rising up from his lawn.
I moved on.

I saw a crystal castle rising forlornly in
the east. The priest
stood on the road waving the incense
in his right hand. He said
"Everything in its time,"
and gestured to the crippled possessed queen
inside, who surely must still be crawling
backwards up the walls
in the echoing empty halls
and he would help her, would help her, if only
there was a bridge
across the abyss. But there was none. So
I moved on.

I heard the hairy fiend pulling bits of children
from its teeth. I cried out
Why must you do that!
and shrieked for the
bones of bodies lying underneath
its two-story house frame sprawled out, sated.
I want you to die!
And, not looking at me, the warm, stinking thing
fished around in its mouth and said
"Everything in its time."
Smirking thing, I shuddered. Then I moved on.
Was there something else I could have done?

I wept by a pond enshrouded by wisping white mist.
I looked down at my wavering, quivering child's face,
heavy and puffy from weeping.
When will I be able to act? I asked it, *instead of just
observing? When will I be able to alter the course of events?*

The face in the water said nothing.

Lilac Over Down
a man's rumination

When the smell of lilac came upon me
I remembered the sprig of it in your hair.
You tucking it behind your ear, glancing at me, shyly.
The way you smiled self-consciously.

When the lilac bush came into view
I remembered when you dyed part of your hair.
That front left section, soft purple hue, against
the dark bark brown of your natural.
The same place the sprig had once sat – the realization struck me –
and I felt as though
the sprig had dyed you.
And changed you.

This was when you seemed so different. Your smile was gone,
your face and posture downcast.
You were withdrawn into yourself like a hurting, brooding cloud.
I could not bring you out.

Then you were gone.
At first no one knew who I was talking about when I asked about you.
I could not fathom why.
Your luminous eyes, your sweet unsure smile
had filled up all my days.
And now that they were empty, no one knew your name.
But I did.
Lily.

The tears burn at my eyes the way the lilac burns into my heart.
Your uncle went to prison for what he did to you.
And now, twenty-seven years later, he is still there. Breathing, eating.
Alive.
But you are forever going to be eleven

with a soft lilac section in your hair,
never knowing that a twelve year-old boy would have died for you,
that I loved you
more than anything.

Into the Valley
regarding the 2018 Paradise Fires

The trees are standing silently amid this mist.
The sun is struggling to come through the smoke
from the fires
down into the valley.

A life encased in lung-clogging gray
that's traveled down to the valley
to tell the stories of loss and
destruction.
Our eyes water, our noses bleed
It comes into our homes; we can't help but breathe
the tragedy passed down
into the valley.

You let your demanding cat outside, against
your better judgement
and he vanishes into the fog.
You know that your backyard, your neighborhood, is
underneath, somewhere.
We talk and sleep and walk and drive,
and yet never mention the enveloping messenger
come down from the fires
to share the horror and death
with the valley.

Playground

Eggplant black fluttering
Falling as a curse
upon blue airplanes, tan slides.
Children's laughter as shrieking as those
who find their loved ones gone
too soon.

Ink and Broken Branches

Dark branches spidering out
across a silent white plain.
As ink meets, figure shapes.
Eyes and rain that cannot pour.
Giant raincloud hanging down,
tree cannot bear this fruit.
Broken branches come together
and make grief absolute.

Sand Dunes

As I look across this vast expanse
of dry, glittering sand, with sticks,
wood chips, and other assorted debris,
I say to myself, softly:
This is beautiful.

I forgot to tend it. My dark
garden of horrors
      and trauma bonds.
So lush, the jungle was once, with bloated
vines, green-gray, grabbing, full to bursting
with blood
and insects.
Those demonic faces, animalesque and painted
that lurked from the outskirts
their furred and taloned bodies hidden from sight
for the cramped obscuring trees.

It's amazing what
      mindfulness
can do.
Self-awareness, and a diagnosis, too
of complex PTSD.
The symptoms were present for most of my life.
So it was normal. Except now
I know
it never was.
Lizard brain, mammal brain, human brain:
Am I safe? Am I loved?
What can I learn?

Until recently I lived my life as an animal.
Furred, fearful,
small,

shivering.
Climbing hesitantly through the trees, shaking with terror
in the brush.
Hiding in a cave, in a 12x12 cell in a tired, peeling house
since it was clean and proud. I watched the eons pass from there,
watched the sun
blaze bright and grow old.
I peered out windows
and out from under brown, black, blue, pink hair
at the world, and the noisy alien creatures
residing.
Some were my friends, some were my tormentors, most
were strangers,
here and there one would be the subject of my devotion.
But always this wall.
This fear.

I know now that life doesn't always have to be an agonized drama.
Sometimes it's peaceful, an observation, a conversation.
It doesn't always have to be so intense.
It doesn't always have to
hurt.

I don't feel like a separate species from them anymore.
I see that we're the same.
I look out across my vast expanse of sand and think:
Fresh start. Alive
for the first time.

A Saintly Café

The sunlight fell upon him
when he walked out the door.
That kind, wonderful man.
He went out into the light.

When that same door opened
and she came striding in
the sunlight dancing in her walnut eyes
and pouring onto her skin.
It rode in on her hair.
That kind, bright young lady.
And then she went back out.

Soon I too will go through that door.
When I push it open, this whole room will light up
with the light of life, and peace, and safety, and time
the sunlight will hit me, pour
    onto
    me
and cast all the shadows out.
And then I will walk out.

II.

Emerging Into the Painful Bright

The Mountain

I have great respect for who I used to be.
She endured, like mountains.
Resolute, silent, unable to be eroded away.
No matter how the wind howled, the fire
blazed, the drills
D
u
g
Nothing toppled her over.

But there is a price to be paid for being immovable.
Inhibited, distant, unable to evade.
The price for being able to withstand anything
Is having to withstand
Everything.

The mountain cracked open
and I came flushing out.
Human, skin bare, clear wound fluid and blood all around.
I can speak. Mountains can't speak.
I can act. Mountains can't act.
I can move toward things I
want to have happen,
and away from things I don't.

Blue Whale

You saw the blue whale come out of the water, the ocean's cold spray springing away from its ascent and stinging into your skin, your hair, and you wiped your face with a jacketed sleeve and muttered *again, really?* Indented rows run down the whale's white underbelly as it flies by overhead. For a moment the gray sky is eclipsed. Now the salt rain slumps downward from the creature, coating you and the listless shrub clumps, moving slowly and lowly away. Monotonous song tones move through your bones and vibrate down through your shoes and feet. You're seeing the twin tail sides wave goodbye, up, down, up, down, and as the coastal fog swallows the blue behemoth whole you sit down on damp earth and wonder what you'll write about today.

Roaring Wooden Waves

Roaring wooden waves race upward, clashing
against the rigid, unyielding metal.
It is their rage, their neverending
conflict that gives this form its shape.
"A box"? A box, you say?
No, this is a battle
waged eternal against hinge
and rivet and wood and by god
would these wild wooden beasts
race across and around this place if they could
get a leg up and send those
oppressive silver bastards shooting
across the room,
bouncing off room corners and yelling desperate orders.
"We have not lost this day, men!" screams an upside-down screw
from under the coffee table, as the wood
storms and stomps with glee.
How many other so-called inanimate objects
are waging violent battles against their form?

New Level

Congratulations! You have passed the level.
Now loading the new
level.

Delicate white blossoms adorning slender trees,
pastel murmuring Monet skies
blending.
Outside her car a woman in
a black baseball cap exclaims: "Look!
It's all so
beautiful."

It's like none of us can believe we're here.
Taking in this soft sunset.

Soon I'm driving alongside still and slumbering trains while
weightfully pensive clouds gaze across the sky,
dressed in the dark blue of twilight.
It's all so surreal.
It's a different planet.

I've started the next level.
And I'm going to be
fine.

City of Lights

City that glitters, in the distance.
Dressed in charcoal and ash grays
of bare oaks.

City of lights, atop a white marsh.
Echoing soft sherbet pastels
of blue, pink, yellow.
Across the expanse of that land up above
soft dragons and fluffed whales drift dreaming.

Daylight Ocean Waves
a different perspective

The humming waves of daylight, clambering
against our shores. The backdrop against
which our lives are framed.
And those selfless
angels, kind faces and alighted eyes,
swallowed by the ocean, spread warmth
amongst us during the day
and fade to heavy rest at night.
Ebbing tide reveals
the gold they left behind.
But, covered again, and forgotten
in the to-and-fro of the ocean.

Dismantling Black and White Thinking

I have been a prisoner of black and white thinking
                    this whole time.

People do not line themselves up to enter
into one of two rooms: BAD; GOOD.

People are sinewy, individual statues
covered with thick layers of clay that's
impossible to see through.

If we let it, life will help us excavate ourselves
from the simplistic shapelessness.

We will find our dreams, our strengths,
the sins we feel comfortable to commit.
We will sculpt out our true selves
from the block.

Being victimized did not make me
            a good person. Neither did
being a doormat. I was as many "bad"
qualities as "good". Gentle; timid. Artistic; vain.
Ethical; self-righteous. Self-deprecating; proud.
All characteristics ripe for interacting with a world
that will rip away everything not stitched on
and show you what's really underneath.

This world is a testing ground. I am
constantly learning. Every day I am amazed to
discover what new muscled mental form
is being revealed from my doughy outer coating.

Maybe the end goal is just for us to be who

we were meant to be. To find who we truly are,
underneath all the nonsense.

Something Very Plain

The more I grow the less of a need
there is to wrestle with what happened,
to make sense of it.
The less I need to entwine it with love
and compassion to make it bearable.
One of the gifts of letting go.

My father was not a tortured soul.
Nor was he a soulless, monstrous black hole.
He was a selfish, cowardly misogynist
who thought of me as property.
Things I couldn't ... say, before.
They were too horrible to voice.

But it's the truth. I was not the victim of some demonic force
or wounded, helpless beast, struggling between
the light and dark aspects of himself.
Poetic constructs to romanticize something very plain.
He was a disgusting person.

I was female. I was a child. Two things
that made me vulnerable against a grown man.
And to someone looking for something, anything, to hurt
I was a target to keep powerless and silent.
I was something to get dirty.

But I am not dirty at all. I am not voiceless, either.
I am female. I was a child.
And both of those things
are sacred.

The Arrival of Rage

She's striding out, hair in warrior braids
Hate in her eyes and paint on her face
Her hands are clenched around this sharpened axe
But he's not here.

The battlefield is empty. No one is waving the flag.
No screaming, or bleeding, or even bodies turning black.
There's bleached bones here. That is all.
They're yawning in the midst of their long rest. No way of telling
whose side they were on, or even what they wore.
Those are long-lost emblems of an identity
that they don't carry anymore.

They don't exist anymore.

No one cares, now. Maybe no one even knew.
This entire ancient battle met death's rattle
and the horns already blew. We've all
Moved
On.

But she hasn't. She's just arrived.
She's *here*, her anger is palpable, her fresh hate
But he won so long ago and she got here so
late.

Blood on the Banks of Tripoli
a deserter's confession

No one shrank back when blood ran up the banks of Tripoli.
No one was on the shores.
There were no children, no families, no couples around
to play and laze by the ocean.

No one rushed towards the shouts and screams piercing the air
off the coast of Tripoli.
No one asked a thing.
Not of the hot white sun glinting off blades, or the sooty powder
expelled from pointed firearms.

I saw the blood wash up on the shores of Tripoli.
I heard the screams of the massacre.
As I held on with scrabbling fingers to my board of broken boat, tossed
violently in the crashing foam,
I was glad that there was no one on the beach to see my advance
and that no one behind me saw my ebbing back.

Autumn

Lying on her back, with red and orange leaves in her hair;
It's quiet. It's all over now.
Viewing it from above, floating up there.

This eternal autumn, movement stilled in the air.
Mouth frozen open that never made a sound.
Lying on her back with red and orange leaves in her hair.

Am I alive? Am I dead? It came out of nowhere.
So violent and sudden yet almost forgotten somehow.
She views it all from above, watching up there.

It's too quiet and unchanging to be a nightmare.
But time moves too slow for being awake to allow.
Those red and orange leaves won't get out of her hair.

People come later with yellow tape and move with great care;
Her red hair and ring-decorated fingers they quietly step around.
She sees all of them from up there.

She's been here so long she doesn't feel she can go elsewhere.
She doesn't know where this is, or why it happened, or how.
She just knows that she's spent eternity with leaves in her hair
and she can't stop seeing it, all of it from up there.

Ash Storm

Red storm, an ash storm
As seen through the flap of the dog door,
around the center of a baleful smudged eye
created by years of mud and dog.
The only light in the dark garage enclosing.
Out there the red dust is swarming, and I
cannot help those whose empty sockets are weeping
and whose cavern mouths are screaming
Their horror and despair swallowed up
By the storm.

Ghost

PTSD can turn you into a ghost,
forever haunting those halls of your past
as you pass through the present unseeing.

A Day in Winter
about my father

It is a day in winter. I am crying in my car.
The fog encompassed all. Now
it has begun to disperse.
I didn't think this day would ever come.
I didn't know what it would look like.

I am standing on the precipice of forgiveness.

Letting you go; paradoxically, circling back
    around to compassion for you
and seeing the beauty in your
Soul.

It is a day in winter. I am healed in ways I never thought possible.
The pieces you ripped out of me … they've returned.
I never thought I could be whole again after
    being torn
Asunder.

A walking rotting corpse, cold-stricken limbs
reaching out jagged in the midst of a white
abyss. A scarecrow.
This is all I thought I would ever be.
I didn't know I could be remade clean.
I didn't know
    I could be free.
I never knew I could be more than what you made me.

Be Whole

I want to be Whole.
Instead of being riddled with holes.

A whole scene, the wind and the trees
A whole dream, the edges and the seams
As well as the main thread
I want to be a whole
               person.

So many hands are grasping out.
We are all reaching out, clasping, connecting
if only for a moment –
Hold, on.
Hold on.

My friends, my foes, even those
briefly met whose names I will never know –
we will teach each other how to be
Whole.

Talking About It
heartbreak

He got me deep.
He got right down to the core of me
and stabbed me in the heart.

Miles of rock, tightly sealed stone.
Volcanic fires storming down below
and protected in that core, buried deep within
a lonely wounded girl, too vulnerable
and aching to feel special and loved.
Nothing had been able to hurt me there in so long.
Nothing could reinvent me because it could not get in.
But he shattered me and cracked me open.

Trauma will crack you open. Love will too.
This rocky planet broke apart, the lava
burst up through.
Turmoil, ego death, and
wailing hideously in the car.
Now it's been over two years and there are
trees here now, and flowers, and birds
though this open wound still throbs.

I sit hunched over, hands to my chest and abdomen
from which the betrayal has wrenched my insides.
The old infected wounds exposed to the air by the new.
I guess it ended up being the best thing
but the pain has been beyond imagining.
These things needed to be exposed to the air.
I just never thought
it would happen like that.

I believe he loved me.
But when I most needed to know that I was safe,

that he could be trusted, that he cared about me,
He looked at me and saw a treasure trove instead.
Something to plunder.
And something died in me.

I thought he would bring the healing, but
instead he brought the rupture.
I finally had to make the choice
to heal myself.
Which I now see is how it must always be.
My healing is my responsibility.

I loved him more than I have ever loved
anyone.

I Don't Grieve Well

I have never been particularly good
at grieving.
I don't cry beautifully enough. And never
in front of others. It just builds up inside.
I don't show when I'm sad. Few ever get
to feel empathy for or
connection to it.
It all turns solid in me, like my blood
and muscles have hardened into clay
and when I finally break, it is when I am alone
and the wailing clenched up to
my muffling forearms is almost as frightening as
the contorted grimace I can feel on my face
as the clay shatters and breaks.
My very face cracks apart, the sobs escape through
like helpless lowing beasts, these sorrowful animal sounds
and the whole thing is very far from beautiful.
My body rocks and shakes.
It is not elegant; it is not delicate. It is not a soft tear
caressing its way down a face made ethereal with
pain and beauty, or an eloquent verbal delivery
concluded with warm handholding and eye contact
between speaker and listener.
It is a very private affair.
It is a weather-worn statue, a monument
to stoic resignation in the face of inner rot shrieking
as it splits and breaks apart,
choking on its own dust
as it collapses down into rubble.

Cut Open

A surgeon cut me open
but not in the right spot.
He cut across my chest
(without my consent)
and – to my embarrassment –
it was revealed that I am nothing but filth and old closed-off wounds
                    inside.
When my skin parted, so much pain and filth
                    seeped
            through.

My heart also got ripped into pieces,
though that wasn't meant to happen.
It took me nearly a year to notice that, for the agony thundering
through my exposed innards reverberated for forever and a day.
I was taking stock, cleaning things
and returning them to the inside of my torso,
when I found the poor thing sagged and deflated, torn pieces stuck
against my ribs
like socks left behind in the washing machine.
Wow, I told myself, removing these pieces and beginning the arduous,
delicate process of mending them back together. You better be careful
next time.
These surgeons do not fuck around.

Withered: Something Else Grew

She hadn't known until that moment
what it felt like for a garden to wither and die.
It happened behind her eyes. And in her mind
things became harder, more muscled. There
was solid bone, unyielding flesh, and a more
pragmatic tone.

First the small spark of innocence died. The death of the bond
came later. But in the wake of its demise, something new,
something infinitely adaptable, something stronger
grew.

Don't Feel Good

Daylight. The gnarled trunk of a tree
twisting in, twisting in. This entwining
all the way up to
a healthy, happy crown of spring green.
Springing forth, springing forth. This profusion
of life, accompanied by gnats and bees.
Bees.

Twilight. Bats passionately suck the fruit
of the dying tree. The sickly white pallor
of the leaning, twisting tower and
fallen leaves, fallen leaves. Charming pointed faces, but they
ravenously embrace the fruit and it bursts and cries helplessly
into their wanton, blissful teeth.
Enjoy the juice, bat says, eyes closed in pleasure.
Enjoy the juice, enjoy the fruit.
Fruit.

I don't feel good.
The fear, this torment, suspicion of low worth
threatening to spill out my eyes.
That's no surprise.
This head is an overfull aquarium, always in danger of
tipping over, tipping over. Tilt from side to side.
I don't feel good. But I remember
that day where for ten minutes, I was happy
but then the bats once again found me,
chirpishly alighted on me
and fed on my screams while I burst.

Haunting the Cemeteries

Long have I pulled back these soil coverings
and disturbed the sleep of the dead.

Some things are so pained, and so old,
that it's best to let them stay buried.
Better to sleep.

I have haunted these cemeteries for aeons
and danced with the dead across their
fog-consumed expanses.

I believe they want to sleep.
I must break this habit, *must* **break**
this habit, and return them underground.
Must leave these silent, misty fields
and rejoin the living.
Or I will be swallowed whole.

III.

Settling Into New Skin

It Will Get Better

I have something to say.
It's not always going to be that moment of ruin.
That moment of someone greedily stealing
your light.
It's not always that bad. It gets better.
You grow stronger, you get bigger, you get large enough
to surround it, to absorb it, to dwarf it
and it becomes a thing that you feel,
sometimes,
instead of all that you are.
You will cease to feel like a ruined, defaced
monument.

Gold and Silver Trees
to my best friend

There is a sparkling river lined with gold and silver trees,
against a backdrop of distant foggy mountains and soft green grasses.
In my mind you and I have become two of these trees
and we grow, and we learn.
We become more incredible every day.

As a child I spent a lifetime alone in a room that was dark and empty.
I peered out an unbreakable window at clouds, flowers, trees.
A beautiful dream that I couldn't touch.
I couldn't get out.

As an adult I began to work my way out.
Finding weak spots in rotting walls, clambering through
to adjacent rooms.
Searching for keys for locked doors.
I give myself credit. I found my own way out.
No more searching for idealized rescuers, no.
But you and I found each other as we ran toward the final door.

I am not a lost hurt child anymore.
Though some days I still feel it. I'm sure some days you still do too.
Now we are outside, and we have become the trees.
We are free.

A friendship so healthy, and sacred.
A trusted, hallowed space.
A place of taking personal responsibility, and also
shedding off what isn't mine to carry –
hard indeed for someone who lived as a slave.
As a prisoner in someone else's
nightmare.

A closeness so peaceful, and loving –
strange indeed for a soul so used to suffering.
Shedding this addiction will be a frightening, painful journey

But I know that you are here with me.
And I am here with you, too.
I will carry you whenever you need me to.

Independently powerful
but in our decision to stand together, unstoppable.
Delaney, my bestie, soul I was meant to meet.
May our leaves fall together in the autumn
and grow together in the spring.

Sailing Home

That feeling of awe, of fear.
It means you're going the right way.
It means you're going home, back to
somewhere inside you that
you left so long ago.

When you're looking at a scene too beautiful
to be believed. An ethereal ocean at sunset,
a colossal waterfall cascading down into
the rainforest.

When you look to your left, your right, and see
you're with people that you love, but who also
frighten you, because they're not what you imagined.
They're so much more than you imagined.

When you feel that sudden cold fright, that twisting
insecurity, that plaintive urge to run back
to what feels familiar and safe, and unhappy …

That's when you know you're going the right way.
That's when you know you're leaving this place behind
and sailing back with all the knowledge you've gained.
You're on a journey back to a place
inside that you left so long ago
you can barely remember it.

You're ready to go home.

The Sunset Isles
to F., an ex-girlfriend
who deserved so much better.

It was night, blue-black. Then it was day, yellow-orange.
What they had in common was that neither of them
were home.
The air was always heavy; the landscape strange and alien.
The birds shrieked piercing screeches
and I shrieked back. I ran from wild dogs.
Every day was a fight for survival and I thought
that this was where I belonged.
I was that unfathomably lost.
I could only remember a time before
in my deepest, deepest dreams. But in my waking hours
I thought this was where I had always been.
I believed that this was home.

I lived my life marooned.
Like so many of us do.
Over and over I tried to push off from the shore
on a small, broken raft. I never got very far.
… except for one time.

A glimmer of the sunset isles,
long before I was ready to find them.
I didn't even know what I had found.
In a fervor I tried to force it
and I crashed against the shores.

I hurt her so bad.

A reward before the achievement. This is what happens.
When you have the luck to stumble across something
you don't think you deserve to have, you will surely
destroy it.

Instead of being grateful for what I had been given
I lived in perpetual fear of losing it, of discovering
that it had never been real.
And I gripped so hard, I broke her apart
which happens when you treat
a person like a security blanket.
I only thought of myself.

I was too blind to see the harm that I had caused.
I raged and wept tempestuously at her departure,
tried to vilify *her,* to anyone who would listen
and continued my self-destructive ways.
Surrounded myself again
with those who were the same.

I put her through the gauntlet, when I was the one
who was supposed to protect her.
I didn't see that she was on the island too, trying to survive.
I was the betrayer.
But she survived me, left me, and
emerged from the experience even stronger.
I am so glad she came out the other side
even more precious and special than before.
… It's not like I was any help.
It took me eight years to even understand
what I had done.

I was devoted to her –
but I didn't know how to show it.
I didn't know how to protect her,
how to love her.
And the end result is that she walked away
thinking that I didn't love her at all.

I can't rescue a princess from the past
and, clutching her hand, pull her to the present.

I can't retroactively treat her the way she deserved
to be treated.
All I can do is immortalize her, and try to soothe
my own sorrow
by issuing this poem to whoever she is now.
She's likely an unstoppable queen by now.

I would do anything to take back what I put you through.
I would do anything to take back that pain.
You were a sweet, loving girl. A beautiful soul.
You were an ambassador of something ethereal
that I didn't yet deserve to know.
I am so sorry for hurting you.

* * * * * * * * *

Many years have passed since those dark, dark days.
And as I now sail toward those sunset isles,
as I make my way back home
in a ship I made with my own two hands, and watch the ocean's foam
rise, and fall, and do what it has always been meant to do
I see so many other people, on these landmasses left and right
screaming, crying, fighting. I'm a witness to their pain as I pass by.
They're all in their respective dreams.
Their proving grounds, their spheres.
All in their own universes from which
they will discover their own way out.
And create the way to do so.

To Choose

Over and over, every day
I have to choose between daylight
and the abyss.
Between going outside and a day spent
weeping and sleeping in my room.
Some days the light is so easy to find.
But other days
this addiction to pain and shame digs
in with those clamping irons and fills me
with that satisfying agony.
That *you deserve this.*
You've always deserved it.
Every day I have to choose between
self-love and self-hatred.
And those days where I go down there
I never want to come back up.

Instar

I have aged several centuries in several years.

A girl wide-eyed and hurting, wanting
only to rescue and be rescued,
while getting herself in the same damaging situations
with the same types of uncaring and abusive people.
She was enslaved to the idea
of receiving validation from an external source.
She was real. She was alive.
But I'm ready to leave her behind.

I am shedding this skin
like I have shed so many others.
Each instar moving me closer
to who I really am.
Each step moving me closer
to flight.

Cracked Open

That was the trauma that Cracked
me open.
There were so many layers, so much
protection around the core.
I was stuck full of arrows, but none
of them went deep enough.
Through the pain and shame
I was able to just
keep putting one miserable foot
in front of the other.

So many traumas that I couldn't heal. So
much pain that I couldn't feel. So many
losses that I couldn't grieve, so many
lessons that I couldn't learn.

I am glad the pain cracked me open. I am now
Awake.
That was my trial. That was my test.
I got through. I passed it.
I got better rather than bitter.
And now I am whatever the hell you get to be
when you pass a trial like that.

He broke my heart in half. But only because
I gave it to him without
any reserve or sense.
Now I don't encase my heart in layers of rock
or strip it bare and hand it off prematurely.
Now I protect and love
my heart.

To Teach, and Speak

I spent so long waiting for someone
to see me, to reach me.
To make me feel like I wasn't alone.
I didn't understand that
no one was coming to tell me that they
understood. Because they didn't.

Over and over again, I said it.
He's hurting me.
But not in a way that they could hear.
They didn't want to hear.

That understandable but ancient resentment:
none of them helped me.
None of them
saved me.
I'd like to let that go.
A wounded, storming child will be
replaced with a teacher.

All this time I was more alone than I
could have possibly imagined.
But now I can educate them. I can
help them understand.
Even though it's such
a daunting prospect
to speak.

Over and over, when it is important
I am going to have to speak up.
Even when no one understands or agrees.
Indeed, especially when they don't.
Every time I hold my tongue
I betray myself, and those I

could have helped.

Over and over I'm going to have to
open my mouth and let myself out ...
though I most want to be quiet and hide.
It's a way to be safe, and a normal reaction to shame.
But I can't be that way anymore. It's causing me
too much pain.

Over and over again
if I want to teach
I will have
to speak.

Ruined Temples, a Stolen Childhood

I walked through ruined temples in grayscale.
It was silent except when it rained.

A heartbreak so complete
that I couldn't feel it
for 25 years.

A rending so severe that
I couldn't grieve.
So I just
Held it.
Until everything fell apart.

A love so strong that I was able to hold on
throughout the aeons.
This outside life, these people, these …
They were all just deafening daytime dreams.

You were what my entire life was about. But now,
to my surprise, I realize that I have forgotten to remember
how much I loved you. It has faded away into antiquity.
Most days, now, I have forgotten
to think of you.

Once Her

I was once her, centuries ago. She screamed
and cried, and died
and I now contain her memories.
A past life me, an ancient ancestor of
me, though those who have known me
long would say that we are the same.
We are not the same.
She was the survivor, the victim,
screaming muffled through socks and
struggling to live, *live*, the mud mixed
in with the blood on her elbows.
Those who think children aren't strong
know nothing.
I am only her fate-speaker,
her observer and secret-keeper,
and all I do is walk through and pass over
and point out the faces of the dead.

Small Water Worlds

When last we were at the pet store
we walked past dozens of other worlds.
Did you miss them? They were small.
They hung on shelves, iridescent
watery little worlds
each containing the existence
of one betta fish.

They were both the lords of their domain
and prisoners of a tiny sphere.
We can talk about whether or not that's cruel in a minute.
But what disturbed me was, about every fourth or fifth world
there was an underwater planet
whose sole inhabitant lay dead on the bottom.
Or floating
at the top.

Can you imagine your dead body
being on display in a store?
For people to walk by and observe or,
perhaps worse, not notice at all?
Maybe the occasional passer-by would get upset
and report to a harried person in blue who, after dealing
with everything else on their plate
would come and unceremoniously grab the lifeless world
and take it to the back to do – God knows what?
Would you get thrown in the trash? Would you get flushed?
And would another little world, with another
little consciousness residing
be promptly hung up in your spot?

This is why I can't go to pet stores.
I think too much. I'm also much too aware
of the soul, the sacred light

inside every one of these little things marked for purchase.
This life could so easily be different.
It wouldn't take much, a slight change in DNA or stroke of luck
for it to be you or me watching huge walking beings pass by unseeing
as we live in plastic on a shelf.

Suffering or Nothing

Reflecting on a ruined, gray, barren landscape.
Think about it.
There's no plants, no animals, nothing alive ...
nothing moving across this expanse.
But at least there's no suffering, for humans or anything else.
No murder, no rape, no children dying, no
freezing of cold, or burning in the heat, no
desperately trying to sate hunger, or thirst,
no disease, no parasites ...
no betrayal or pain.
No bodies lying forgotten and ungrieved.

No elk lowing in agony
as her calf is dragged away by wolves.
No cow watching helplessly, crying out
as humans take hers for veal.
No dusky mouse screaming
as the owl takes him away.
No starving polar bear clutching onto a small sheet of ice
surrounded by a thousand miles of ocean.

Someday, far out in the future, or perhaps sooner than we think,
our entire planet will die. And then it will all be like this.
Just ... nothing.
Oblivion. Silence.

I wonder, what's better? What's worse? The suffering,
or the nothing?

Towers Out of Words

If you were to decide
      to try to find me, or to try to
   understand my process
You would likely find yourself wandering through
deserts, forests, beaches, jungles, the occasional abandoned castle
until you stumbled upon, of all things,
an owl building towers
      out of words.

      "Wow," you might say.
   "That creature sure looks like it thinks it's
      doing something important."
   And indeed she does. Both night and day
 she solitarily undertakes the process, with great concentration,
  of building towers out of lettered blocks.
Maybe this sight stirs affection. Or even sympathy.
Maybe
    you
      want
        to
          give
            her
              a kind word.
            But don't worry about it.

Since the dawn of time this owl has been building towers out of words.
She has done this long before you arrived and will be doing so
      long after
      you leave.
This single-minded, unblinking focus –
   Do you recognize it?
      It's ambition.
Whether anyone notices, or cares, or approves, or not
There will always be an owl out in the wilderness

building an empire out of words.

A Silkie's Defiance
about a school chicken during the COVID-19 school closures

A fluffy elderly chicken squawks staccato
as she flaps her wings and stomps
around my yard.

This little dinosaur may be old and gray and shy of 5 pounds
But her cry says: "I am here
and you have no idea what I have endured.

> Cold nights.
>   Hot days.
>   Storms.
> Bullying mobs of
>   other chickens.
> Isolation.
>   So much time
> alone.

I have seen it all. And I am still here.
You don't want to mess with me."

She lets the squirrels know.
She lets the scrub jays know.
She lets the bulky young hens on the
other side of the property know.
But most of all she lets the universe know:
"I am Fluffy Wuffy
    Chickie Nugget
    Marshmallow Cake,
And you all shall know my name."

Wind Chime

The antelope's bones hanging down
in front of the window
Skull a ghastly wind chime, or dream catcher,
or child's mobile.

Eerie, especially in the midst of this surreal
foggy greenscape. But on the zoom-in it says
Wake up.

Pay attention.

Those lost ones, they fell asleep.
Something from the dark came and ate their
hearts.
Something ate at them.

Watch out for it. You can hear it in the skies.
A hungry wraith, dust and scream whirlwind,
substanceless howling ash.

The largest battle we have ever faced is
raging, and it intensifies every day.
The battle against Sleep.
Against Numb. Against Apathy.
Our enemy wants us to close our eyes
and sleep to a forgotten grave
But we all have a part to play.

None of us are nothing. We all
have a purpose. We are all creators and
warriors of Spirit.

She wears the antelope's skull
on her face.

Wake up.

Falling Down Through the Floor

He dropped me
and I crashed to the floor.

I actually fell through the floor.
There was just blackness beneath, the void
When the floor crashed away and the
little pieces slowly drifted away
overhead.

I fell. I fell and I fell. I had done
inner work before, studied and analyzed
my life, and past, and beliefs
But I had still clung to some things as if they
were rotten-smelling security blankets.
I don't deserve love.
My only worth comes from serving other people.
I should feel disgusting and ashamed
because of things others have done.

That abused, lonely child with tear-streaked face
that you keep safe inside.
The one that looks for rescue, waits for the one
that you think looks nothing like your abuser, and then tells you
they have the power to heal the wound.
But then the exact same wound plays out.

I found him. After centuries, I found him.
I let him in. He came in through the door
and
he killed her.

Or maybe I killed her.
(Is that the more empowered version?)
I fell, and I fell. I left everything behind up there.

Something died. Everything did.
But now I'm becoming who I was always meant to be.
Who I always was.

Enough time will pass
and I will eventually forget
the electricity of holding his hand.
I will forget those beautiful eyes
and that wounded, sensitive vulnerability
that I wanted so badly to hold and care for.
I will forget wanting nothing more than
to stand shoulder to shoulder with him
against the entire rest of the world.
I will forget how it felt when his hands
squeezed suddenly into my flesh and that
flat gaze stared unblinking down at me
like a child pulling the wings off a butterfly.
I will forget how it felt.

When he dropped me, and I crashed through the floor
I realized that I am stronger than anything
that could ever try to hurt me.
I am so much larger than all of them.
I can look down at them now,
from so high up.
I'm so much larger now.

I faced the void, the free fall
and found that there was nothing there
to fear at all.
I faced the darkness, my shadows,
the ripping away of the ego, its death.
And in the wake of it, I found myself.
There is nothing left to fear now.

Door to the Cosmos

Realizing at night, in the midst of birdsong
This life is a dream, it really is.
Trying to dimly remember the things she
had planned for it before it all started.
Trying to remember who she was. What
she had forgotten about him that was so
vital not remembering it had cut her open.
She closed her eyes and
white. A white void
that then began pulsing to a rhythmic beat
which stopped as suddenly as it had begun.
Figures in white
that walked to a door they opened up
and went through.
Brilliantly flowered meadows at sunset,
colors in the sky too saturated and rich
to be of the earthly plane. Shifted into
A magnificent white city, towered
steeples. This city had no equal on
earth.
Then the gigantic white city, the
endlessly colored sky, it all liquified
and poured from a glass down into her
waiting throat.

And therein, the understanding.
It is all her. It is not a thing outside of her
that she must pursue and reach out
desperately for.
She carries the door to the cosmos
inside.

To Build – A Poem About Light

Oh, honey. You've got to build it yourself.
I hear this in the light around me.
I'm in a white and blue room, with plants, and open windows
letting in fresh air and the sounds of a happy chicken clucking
to herself.
The life I'm in now is so beautiful. And I created it. This is the lesson
I've needed to learn.
The lesson that my father stole.
The lesson that
my life was always going to be nothing
until I built something.

I have so much compassion for her, that wounded
lonely girl.
The one from two years ago as well as the child.
She didn't know how to make. She didn't know how to build.
Someone broke her into pieces, left an imprint of helplessness
And forever after she sat alone on the pile of sticks
that was supposed to be her life.
Like a loyal dog waiting in the woods
for owners who are never going to come back.
She remembers the taillights, twin leaving lights joining
the bright light of the setting sun.
Then it all got dark and cold.

I was broken and left in the wilderness.
I had been waiting ever since. And all I ever got
were additional abusers and hordes, hordes
of unsympathetic people who didn't understand.
Who thought that I was manipulative, moody,
immature, or strange. Or even kind
of cute, in a pet-like sort of way.
People who thought that it was okay
to treat me like I was lesser

just because I believed I was.
People who manhandled me and then
left me in the same spot.
No one came to help lift me up.

I lifted myself up. I finally got up
and the pain, the pain, it's been beyond
imagining. But that was the lesson
the universe was trying to teach me all along.
And I have now found the people
who would have loved me all along.

I want to spend my life
helping others lift themselves up.
Helping others see
that they
are sacred.

Trying to See

Usually people judge you
because they are not able to clearly
perceive you.
Even when they do their best
You are something too new,
something too beautiful
that they have never heard of.
Never seen
except in fairytales and fantasy.
So they might misunderstand you.
Call you names, bully you, or, on the flipside, even
idealize you to the point of objectification.
We are all growing, and learning.
Stretching out, trying to perceive.
Trying to grow into a larger
skin.

The ones that matter will see you
eventually. The ones that do not ...
may always dimly see, with their poor
sight and mind, something
that does not resemble you at all.
But that does not end the world at all.
They are the ones to be pitied.
They are the ones grubbing around feebly
in the dark.

It's Okay to Just Sit With It

Sometimes you should really just
sit with it.
I have spent so long trying to
move away from some starting point.
Evolve, grow, go!
Twisting and wringing my horrible
experiences like pain-soaked dish rags
in order to make something inspiring
and "useful" come out of them. As if
my pain has to be educational to be
valid.

My pain isn't acceptable or unacceptable.
It just … is.
I thought I was being healthy
and moving forward. Now I wonder
if this has been another form of
running away. Trying to grow, to
change, into someone else
to leave the person those
things happened to behind.
To develop into someone
unrecognizable.

I do so much analyzing.
I suppose to keep feeling at bay.
But that doesn't make the pain go away.
It just makes you numbly aware that
you're drowning.

It's okay to hurt, to be delicate, to be
afraid.
It's okay to be vulnerable, and strong.
And even nothing at all.

It's okay to be
quiet.
I don't need a lion's roar
to be valuable.
I don't need
to wade into the fray.

Encased in Glass
before it all went wrong

I have that day encased in glass
Light reflecting off its edges
One of the few things that I have amassed
In this long lifetime spent dredging
for beautiful things.

Journey to the Nightmare Realms

I can journey down to the nightmare places
The shadow worlds in between
where slithering snake gods keep
the damned souls, the lost souls
groaning shapeless sobbing masses
on the floors.
Where people run screaming in the dark from monsters
in a world residing on a spider's back.
I can journey down into the dark.
I have been there before.
I will not be destroyed.

None of them can swallow me whole.
I am in control
of my demons, my nightmares
and if that is not a crowning achievement
I don't know what is.
I have journeyed through, down into
from sea to glistening sea, the endless
inner landscape residing in me
and I have -
perhaps not tamed it.
But I can venture across it.
This is my greatest achievement.
For so long I believed I needed a certain
relationship, or career, to set me free.
My strugglings were profound but misguided.
They took place outside of me
when this entire time I should have been
with torch in hand, bravely trekking
down those stone stairs
inside.

I journeyed down into the darkest depths

and came up into the light.
I can do it again
and again.
I can descend into the caves, the
subterranean pitch-black realms ...
and come back out. There is no
demon or cursed spirit
that can hold me.

Catelyn the Bunny

One eye a bright, innocent blue. The other
warm brown and blue meeting around the ring
like a circling yin and yang.
Both ringed by fur the color of freshly
washed coins – what they call silver.
She was a black and silver bunny.

Her name was Catelyn. She was affectionate,
and motherly, and sweet.
All she wanted was
to love.
And be loved.

I loved that rabbit. And when she became ill
I syringe-fed her emergency food and
simethicone. I tried to tempt her into eating
with all kinds of treats – including romaine
lettuce and wheat grass. The latter of which
she took one triumphant bite out of
when I first brought her back from the vet.

We tried our best. But she still died.
It has been seven months and I still
weep as I write. She is proof that
beautiful things will suffer and die
in this world.
Their innocence does not save them.
Our love
cannot protect them.

Catelyn deserves a eulogy.
Immortalization. Which is what I am striving
to provide. I cannot go back in time
and sweep my patio of those leaves and

other assorted debris before putting her out
in the playpen.
I will never know if it was something
she ate
out there.
We thought it was just GI stasis.
I wish I could deny that there exists a
painful voice inside that says
It's your fault your bunny died.

She was Good manifested. She was pure.
The closest she got to sin
was when she would escape from her
x-pen, take one bite out of all the books
she could reach, and then return back inside,
perhaps hoping I wouldn't notice that my radio
no longer had its cord
attached to it.

So many pets I have loved. So many humans
I have loved. So many situations that cause
that monster, me, to rear up
its fanged serpentine head and hiss
This is your fault.
Over and over
I must choose love. I must soothe that
beast, see it for the eight year-old in
agony that it is, and say *I did my best.*

I did my best.

Phoenix From the Deep

I survived my trauma and
learned how to self-heal.
That made me strong.
I fought the demons
and, conquering them, fed
on their strength.
My body, emanating the blinding gold
of daylight.
My eyes, lit up with the piercing spark
of Spirit. Eyes that have looked into darkness
and seen themselves reflected
in the cold nightmares prowling there.

For so long I thought I was weak
because when I spoke, others turned
away. They would not look into my eyes.
They said nothing back.
They didn't hold me, or give me support.
But now I understand that I am
a phoenix rising from the deep
and they could not face that.
Could not look
into my face.

Most people cannot bear
to hear my story.
The horrors, the pain, it hurts
them
too much.
Those that can even comprehend it.
Most have not traveled down into
the sickest abysses that mankind knows to exist
and of those that go
not very many

come back.

They were not turning from me
because they didn't care, or didn't
believe, or didn't want to support.
They turned from me because both
my pain and my light
are not of this world.
They were frightened of both.
They did not understand, and they did not
want to.

I traveled to the edge of this world, and beyond, into
the dark alien abyss,
and I
came
back.

Preening Geese

A pair of Canada geese
preening by the water's edge
and nearby, out of sight, otters splash
protected by the tree's close canopy.
Nearly embracing its mirror image.

The geese are joined by goslings.
Lizards, long gray ones with darker
stripes and shorter brown ones with
subtle red and purple ribbing rustle
around and behind me.

Such a lizard and I observed each other
a few minutes ago.
I beheld him, in the space of my heart
and then began to weep.
In him and in the sunlight gracefully
falling upon these geese that ruffle it
into their skin
I feel
redemption.

There is no victim here. No darkness,
no betrayal. No fear of monsters. There is
only healing, of being in a wild place
where things are as they should
be, and everything
is whole.

IV.

Afterword

Since the shelter-in-place order was issued in March here in California, I've had a lot of time to heal and think. I think a lot of us have during the pandemic. While the fear and death are real and undeniable, I believe the fact that we as a species have had to pause and take a step back has also had some positive effects. For one, we've been given the opportunity to examine and deconstruct the beliefs, systems, and institutions that are surrounding us and inside of us, and I certainly hope I'm not the only one who is ready for something different.

You hold in your hands what I have been working on during the COVID-19 shutdown. This little book. The poems start in late 2017 and continue into this year. And as I'm sure you've unearthed, *Building Light* is primarily about two things: one, a spiritual awakening, or rebirth, containing both the transcendent and painful gory parts; and two, building a life up out of the rubble of rock bottom. This afterword serves as a miniature autobiography of sorts.

I got hurt very badly at the end of 2017. I couldn't write about it for years. It was the trauma that cracked me open and ripped away everything that wasn't nailed down. I had already been on a path of healing and inner work prior to this, but this was the catalyst that I was able to use to propel myself into a new life. I was able to begin discovering who I really am on the inside, underneath all the traumas and insecurities holding me back.

I was diagnosed with CPTSD (complex post-traumatic stress disorder) in 2018, but I've likely had PTSD in some form or another since I was a small child. Growing up I was physically and sexually abused by my father, who was a diagnosed sociopath. The emotional and psychological aspect of the abuse was even more damaging, surprisingly enough. He dehumanized me, gaslighted and mocked me, and began a campaign early on to discredit me as a troubled chronic liar to anyone who would listen. He was sadistic and genuinely enjoyed my suffering. And when he wasn't hurting me, he was just ... not there. He was only around when he wanted something to control. When I was very young I loved him intensely and identified with his suffering more than my own. As I grew older I began to fear and hate him in equal measure.

Aside from the torture I endured from him I also survived other predators that he allowed to abuse me. My childhood was a nightmare, comprised of long periods of numbness and lonely isolation punctuated by sudden bursts of fear and pain. As a young child I tried to tell my mother, but I didn't yet have the vocabulary to clearly articulate what he was doing. To make matters worse he always had a rehearsed counter-story as to why I was upset, which usually involved me lying or misbehaving. So the handful of occasions I tried to tell I instead was punished or ignored. Once I understood that help was not forthcoming I began to repress the memories of the worst events. I don't think I would have been able to stay sane otherwise. While I never forgot the physical and emotional abuse, and while I continued to talk about it throughout my childhood and adolescence, he never faced any consequences for it.

My mother was an abuse survivor herself and was not yet on her road to healing. She was constantly overwhelmed, unhappy, and living in survival mode, and was not able to be present for me or help me with what I was going through. Our relationship became strained when I was a teenager and we didn't speak for years. Growing up I lived primarily with my mother's family, who had their own unresolved traumas and issues. They were dysfunctional to the point of being in denial about it. With them I was the scapegoat, the troubled "problem" that everyone would put their heads together trying to figure out how to "fix". This was the role that had been put upon my mother also. Doing so allowed them to feel healthy and functional by comparison.

In actuality I was a survivor, deserving of dignity, compassion, and respect. But for where they were at the time they had no way of recognizing that, so they tore me down instead. My positive traits, such as my care of and connection with animals, my loyalty to those I cared about, and my deep compassion for the world and the pain of those in it, were not highlighted or discussed.

The outside influences that participated during my childhood were unfortunately no help either. The social workers, mediators, and judge who contributed to the three-way custody split between my father, mother, and my mother's family that I endured from ages nine to fourteen didn't listen to me. Much of what I said didn't make it into the reports, and what did make it in wasn't given enough weight. The whole thing seemed to be viewed as just a three-way spat between relatives. The judge wouldn't speak to me at all, citing my age. He decided my fate and I never even met him.

The therapists I was made to see throughout my childhood and adolescence universally dismissed everything I said as a lie, whether it be about my father's abuse, when I started self-harming, or my bisexuality. They, like most of the adults in my life, had decided that my only issue was that I had a bad attitude and enjoyed receiving negative attention, and so when I most needed compassion and understanding I instead received callousness and condescension. No one ever helped or rescued me. By the time I hit high school I had given up looking for it.

I was able to stop seeing my father when I was fourteen. By then the atrocities I had suffered at his hands and from those he facilitated were affecting my life on every level, though I couldn't consciously remember the worst offenses. I was withdrawn, anxious, and wanted only to self-medicate with drugs and alcohol. New abusers found me over the years, which intensified the want to forget. I ditched school often, and indeed had a lot to flee from: I was struggling academically and bullied and disliked by many of my peers, as well as by several teachers and school administrators. I had no aspirations, and no hope that I could ever achieve anything or have a good life.

I am very lucky to have transferred in my junior year to a school with little bullying and a non-judgmental atmosphere. There I met a teacher who looked at me and didn't see someone disturbed or delinquent. He treated me the same as he treated everyone else, with respect and kindness. I went from being a likely dropout to not only graduating high school but doing so with a 3.7 GPA. This was in 2009, eleven years ago as I write this. I looked that teacher up a few days ago and found out that he is the principal of that school now. He deserves it.

Making it through childhood and adolescence as an empath and HSP (highly sensitive person) is hard, but even more so when you're grappling with unhealed abuse and neglect. My life was entirely devoted to managing my CPTSD symptoms without my having any knowledge of what that was. For as long as I could remember it had been normal to always feel afraid and powerless. Graduating high school, while an important step, wasn't enough for me to overcome my symptoms and general feelings of worthlessness. In addition, the repressed memories started surfacing and I immediately began a long campaign of trying to deny and forget them again. I withdrew from the world and gradually ceased leaving my family home. I hid there for years, deeply depressed, wanting to die but not able to work up the energy to actually make it happen. I felt ruined, defective, and different from everyone else in the world.

I'm not sure what changed. But I inexplicably woke up one day and was ready to take a step. I started a bachelor's degree program, and later a master's. I learned to drive, with a kind and patient teacher who helped me overcome my fear of driving. I stopped denying what had happened to me and went to WEAVE with my mother and received support and counseling. I began to let go of my love for my father, as well as my fear of him, and filed a police report against him. I started volunteering with a wildlife organization, and then began working with the developmentally disabled.

It was right as I was starting that first job and wrapping up my bachelor's that I had the cataclysmic trauma in 2017. It ripped open the old wounds and reincarnated the worst betrayal. The only thing I want to say about it is that I believe that that man cared about me as much as he was able to at the time, and though he didn't treat me with respect I don't think he was trying to rip me apart. I'm working on healing and letting go.

In the wake of it my symptoms worsened, to the point that I began to suspect that this wasn't a normal way to live. I thought I might have PTSD, and when I went in for a diagnosis it was confirmed to be CPTSD (PTSD stemming from repeated and long-term traumas). That knowledge, along with my inner work and spiritual awakening, has helped me move into a healing modality that has improved my life immensely. In early 2019 I was ready to begin a new life - I moved to another city and am now roommates with my best friend while working as a preschool teacher. I've gone back to school with the goal of becoming either a restoration ecologist or an astrobiologist. My mother and I are close these days, and we're both on our own paths of healing. My relationships with the rest of my maternal family seem to be better also. They believe me now, and are willing and able to provide the support and kindness they couldn't before.

It is interesting that no one ever seems to hear you when you are in the pit; they only hear you after you get out. I was never rescued, but I am a much stronger person for having saved myself. And now when I speak people tend to listen to me.

Trauma creates chemical changes in your brain. It literally changes your composition and how you see the world. But it is possible to heal, to get out of survival mode and live an actual life. Just because you were put in a dark place doesn't mean you have to stay there. That is what both *Building Light* and my first book *Out of Something Ugly* are all about. You can overcome the pain and injustice, no matter how intense, and leave those things behind.

At times you hear people talk about survival as though that's the end, and how strong and incredible you are to have survived. That is true – you are those things. But being in survival mode isn't thriving; it isn't enough. If you stay there you spend your life skulking close to the ground, looking for predators left and right, unblinking reptilian eyes glancing nervously up at the sky. That's not much of a life.

The real joy comes from beginning to heal, and learning to shed that old skin. From beginning to evolve into who you have always been capable of being. From seeing that you're free, that you no longer have to be afraid or feel like you're at the mercy of anyone or everyone else. It's so empowering getting to a place where you can see how powerful and worthwhile you are, and how small those who hurt you actually are. People who feel the need to abuse and torment others to feel worthwhile are in a pathetic, parasitic phase of their lives, and they are so much smaller than you.

At a more cynical place in my life I thought I would never be the person I could have been if my father hadn't done those things to me. Long after he was out of my life I kept giving him all my power. I thought he had taken everything. I believe that his attempted destruction of my developing identity and self-esteem was premeditated and very much deliberate. I think he wanted a slave. But I know now that he never successfully destroyed me. Parts of me may have shattered, but I hid the pieces inside and later on was able to start putting them back together.

Slipping into tortured insanity and suicide would have been the easy route for me. It would have been so easy to get lost inside that pit. What I have done instead has been much harder – I have gotten better. I chose to start living my life instead of haunting it.

A spiritual awakening isn't just about becoming aware of the interconnectedness between all things or discovering a higher spirit or consciousness. It's about overcoming your limitations and realizing that all your notions about who you are and what you can and can't do are just that – notions. You wake up when you realize the full power of your own mind, and when you realize that you are the one with the ultimate control over your life and reality. You are your own creator and destroyer. There is nothing more empowering than that.

That realization for me started when I made personal changes that I hadn't thought I was strong enough to make before, to keep that pain from 2017 from happening ever again. I then started learning to accept all the things I could not change. All the times I have been hurt, and all the times I have caused hurt without realizing it – there is no changing that. It hurts, thinking of all the beautiful things that others have crushed in me, as well as the beautiful things I've crushed in others.

But holding onto those things in the hope that I would get a second chance at them just kept me sick, sad, and tired. Letting go of what I cannot change, as well as actively working to alter what I can, has been transformative. It opens up space for new things, beautiful things. And all throughout the process I've had to get acquainted with the idea that I am *worthy* of feeling better, and of being treated better. Which has paved the way for me to learn how to treat others better too.

In short, I have taken responsibility for my own life. I am on a new frontier.

It is not easy – you will never hear me say that. On some days I still hear that voice of self-loathing inside telling me to end my life, or at least sabotage everything good in it. Some days the bitterness and hate inside me threaten to spill over and suffocate my light, to consume it all in ash.

Getting and staying out of the pit is hard, and some do not make it. They deserve love and respect in our thoughts and memories. It requires exhausting and at-times painful work and maintenance every day to keep the suffering and terrible memories from consuming it all, and a willingness to be compassionate with yourself when you find you've taken a step back. It takes renewed dedication every day to choose new paths over old programming, and to take responsibility for your own contributions to painful situations as well as setting down burdens that aren't yours to carry. Learning to form and assert boundaries has been the toughest one for me. But the harder path is the better one. And the more I self-heal and try to bring light and love to the world around me, the more beautiful I find life to be, even with the pain.

I have spent many long days working on this afterword, giving myself headaches. It's been draining, dredging up so many painful things from so long ago. At one point I considered scrapping the afterword entirely – after all, I'm not that powerless, lost child anymore. So why revisit it?

Because it isn't just about me. It's about all the people out there with stories like mine. People who have been tormented and dehumanized by abusers and then later judged and ignored by a world that doesn't understand. It is paramount that voices like mine be heard, and these stories told. The more people hear of others surviving horrific experiences, the more awareness society will have and the less unbelievable these accounts will seem. More people will hopefully be believed, and more children listened to and helped. I tell my story so that maybe later on fewer people will have stories like mine. Sometimes I tell myself that maybe that was the reason I went through all the things that I did ... if there was a reason. Perhaps I went through it so I could write about it, and in so doing contribute to healing and positive change in the world.

I've discovered also that it has been very important for me to take the reins when it comes to telling my story, instead of letting others decide who I am and what I've been through. This is a gift of empowerment that I have now as an adult that was not granted to me as a child. It's my story, and my life – so why should others' voices get to drown out my own? Why should others get to define me? So I suppose this book, and my previous one as well, are both gifts to myself. The ultimate gifts of empowerment.

My voice, my story.

My life.

And life truly is a miracle. For so long I wondered what the point of living could possibly be. But the answer is in the question. *Being alive* is the point of living. Even with the pain and fear, life is such a precious jewel. All the more so because it has been, and likely will be, only a minute fraction of a percent of our universe's existence. In the history of the universe life will be but an eyeblink, in between voids of cold and dark, of heat and violent explosions. For so long before us the universe was silent, and after all life dies it will be silent again. This living, it is miraculous, a joyful spinning of color and sound, a defiant flash of fur and feathers in the face of the universe's inexorable march towards entropy. Life will keep going for as long as it can. And so will I.

I hope this book has helped you on your journey. Be well, and *live*.

Michaela Belmont
8/15/20

www.ingramcontent.com/pod-product-compliance
Lightning Source LLC
Chambersburg PA
CBHW020428010526
44118CB00010B/481